W9-AOJ-254

Environmental
AMERICA

Environmental
AMERICA

The Northeastern States

by
D.J. Herda

The Millbrook Press
Brookfield, CT
The American Scene

Cover photographs courtesy of D. J. Herda

Inside photographs courtesy of Tom Stack & Associates: 19; U.S. Environmental Protection Agency: 23, 34, 48; U.S.D.A. Forest Service, Barry Nehr: 44; U.S. Department of Energy, 37; D.J. Herda: 6, 9, 10, 13, 15, 20, 28, 32, 42, 50

Designed by Moonlit Ink, Madison, WI 53705
Illustrations by Renee Graef

Cataloging-in-Publication Data
Herda, D. J.
Environmental America: The Northeastern States.
Brookfield, CT, The Millbrook Press. 1991.
64 p.; col. ill.; (The American Scene)
Includes bibliographical references and index.
Summary: The impact of humankind and society on the environment, with special emphasis on the Northeastern region
ISBN 1-878841-06-8   639.9 HER

1. Northeastern states—environmental impacts—juvenile literature. 2. Conservation of natural resources. 3. Pollution. [1. Environmental America: The Northeastern States] I Title. II. Series.

CONTENTS

INTRODUCTION

Northeastern America must have seemed a mecca to early colonists. Its rolling hills and countless lakes, rivers, and streams echoed with the calls of wildlife—loons and ducks and teals; beavers and wolves and deer; turkeys and hawks and owls. The trees were a living canopy of green, extending from the shores of the Atlantic Ocean to the highest peaks of the Appalachian Mountains and beyond.

The Northeast is made up of several different environments. The northernmost range of the region boasts mile after mile of second- and third-growth pine tree forests. Maine, Vermont, West Virginia, and New Hampshire have some of the largest. The coastal wetlands, with their sandy shores and wave-swept beaches, make up part of the environment of eastern Massachusetts, Rhode Island, New Jersey, and southeastern Connecticut, while rolling hills and thick hardwood forests cap much of upstate New York and Pennsylvania.

OUR EARLY ANCESTORS

The American Northeast is different today from what it was when our earliest ancestors walked the Earth. Nearly 2 million years ago, a hominid species of animal called Homo erectus evolved specialized behaviors that enabled it to use the wealth of the grasslands more efficiently than any other species before. Hominids had been hunting small animals with sticks and stones for hundreds of thousands of years. But Homo erectus took the process one step further.

As our ancestors learned to hunt in packs, they were able to stalk and kill large game. As they learned to control fire, they gained the ability to drive game, repel predators, cook their food, and control vegetation. They eventually extended their range outside tropical climates. Before long, Homo erectus had spread from Africa to China and then north to central Europe.[1]

(opposite page)
The northeastern states boast some of the most scenic natural environments in the nation.

This geological era, known as the Pleistocene epoch, was a time during which much of the world was covered with vast glaciers. These huge ice packs advanced and retreated regularly. As the glaciers retreated, the lands blossomed with magnificent animals now able to travel far to the north. Ancestors of modern-day lions, today confined to the African grasslands, once ranged as far north as present-day Alaska. Rhinoceroses, elephants, camels, and horses thrived throughout North America.[2]

NEW SPECIES EVOLVES

About 90,000 years ago, a new species of hominid evolved, probably from Homo erectus. Homo sapiens had a larger brain and may have been the first hominid to use language, allowing it to hunt more efficiently and increase in numbers.

By 50,000 years ago, much of North America's native fauna, including saber-toothed tigers and giant ground sloths, had disappeared. One of the reasons was probably a changing climate; another was the unchecked growth of sprawling deserts. But the greatest reason may have been Homo sapiens' increasing skill as a hunter. Our modern ancestors had become so efficient at killing certain species that they very likely wiped out entire populations of animals.

The disappearance from the continent of large game animals created drastic changes in human culture. People moved less often from place to place and became more sedentary. They usually changed their life-styles to adapt to their surroundings. Occasionally, however, they changed their surroundings to adapt to their life-styles.

Humans began living in permanent settlements and keeping domesticated animals and pets. They developed agriculture in low-lying river valleys. There the climates were mild and the soils were rich and easily cultivated with such primitive tools as sticks and plows. Before long, civilization was born.[3]

It didn't take Homo sapiens long to leave its mark on the environment. With its superior brain and strong will to survive, the species soon made more of an ecological impact than any other creature since the beginning of life. By the early

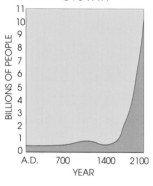

World Population Growth

BILLIONS OF PEOPLE

11
10
9
8
7
6
5
4
3
2
1
0

A.D.   700   1400   2100
YEAR

World population growth and global development are two of the main problems facing the environment.

Sources: Population data from Population Reference Bureau, various publications; historical data from Richard D. Lamm, *Hard Choices* (Denver, CO: May 1985), p. 34

1700s, much of the American Northeast was beginning to show signs of human abuse.

Today, for the first time in history, the plant and animal species that inhabit the Earth—including Homo sapiens—are in serious danger of destruction.

A country road and covered bridge are two examples of human-kind's encroachment on nature.

THE LAND WE WALK

Despite the early destruction of its natural habitat, the Northeast boasts a variety of wildlife—from deer and black bears to red and gray foxes, coyotes, great barred owls, bluejays, mourning doves, finches, and humpback whales.

Most of this wildlife lives and thrives in the sparsely settled areas of the region. Far fewer species live around the more heavily populated, industrialized areas of New York, New Jersey, Pennsylvania, and Washington, D.C.

One of the reasons, of course, is that animals don't usually live where people live. Most wildlife instinctively seeks the wilderness for its own protection from humans, thus ensuring its own survival and that of its species.

Another reason is that animals don't live where their natural habitat has been damaged or destroyed. Faced with commercial development, wildlife moves farther and farther from civilization in an endless search for suitable feeding, nesting, courting, and breeding sites.

Nor do animals live with pollution—or, at least, not for long. When chemical poisons from industrial smokestacks fall to Earth, they create various chemical and physical reactions. The chemistry of the soil changes, affecting plants' ability to grow. Inland lakes and streams turn stagnant, killing off aquatic life. And the food chain—that delicately interwoven web of life—begins to break down.

(opposite page)
Even in the "country," humankind's intrusion on the environment can be found in roadways and electrical power lines.

THE BALANCE OF NATURE

Imagine for a moment a glass terrarium—a self-sustaining mini-environment. Inside the terrarium are soil, bacteria, green plants, root-eating worms, worm-eating lizards—both male and female—and moisture. The terrarium sits in a west-facing window, where it receives an average amount of sunlight. Assuming you left the terrarium totally untouched, how long do you think the community of life inside would survive? One week? Two weeks? A month?

Actually, terrariums are capable of regenerating themselves indefinitely. All the ingredients for life are present—moisture from the soil and respirating plants, oxygen, carbon dioxide, soil nutrients, bacteria to convert dead plant life into nutrients, and worms and lizards capable of reproducing as required.

What would happen, though, if someone opened the terrarium and treated the soil with an insecticide to kill the worms? Without worms, the lizards would soon die. Without lizards, the amount of nutrients being returned to the soil would gradually decrease. The physical and chemical composition of the soil would change, making life for the plants more and more difficult until eventually they would die, too. Without plants, the moisture would soon disappear. Before long, what was once a growing, thriving microcosm of life on Earth would be a dry lump of hardened dirt.

OUR DIMINISHING HABITAT

The Earth is very similar to a sealed terrarium hurtling through space. Like the terrarium, it contains various gases necessary to sustain life, plus bacteria, plants, soil, worms, and lizards—and, of course, tens of millions of additional plant and animal species.

(opposite page)
All of nature is closely interrelated–from the lowest life forms to the highest.

Yet we continue treating our planet like the person who deliberately abused the terrarium. As a result, plants and animals are disappearing from the Earth at an astounding pace. Many varieties of beneficial insects and burrowing animals have already disappeared from beneath northeastern soils. With them have gone a large number of predators such as badgers, foxes, hawks, owls, eagles, coyotes, and timber wolves. Numerous species of aquatic life have disappeared from northeastern coastal waters. If something isn't done soon to change things, we, too, will be faced with the prospect of trying to live on an uninhabitable planet.

THE ENERGY TRAP

One of the Northeast's greatest environmental polluters is the energy industry. Throughout Pennsylvania and other areas of the region, great deposits of coal have been mined to produce fuel to power America's lights, factories, and vehicles. But extracting that coal to meet our nation's rising energy demands has proven costly, time-consuming, and sometimes even fatal.

Coal in northeastern states such as Pennsylvania, New York, and West Virginia is most often extracted by a method known as underground mining. This method employs deep tunnels burrowed into the earth to expose and extract hidden seams of subterranean coal.

The main environmental problem with underground mining is that the tunnels often result in the leaching of minerals, toxic chemicals, and other solutions used in mining into nearby soils. This changes the soils' chemical makeup and destroys native plants and croplands—sometimes permanently. In addition, some of the chemicals leach into nearby waterways, killing off aquatic plants and animals. Others infiltrate underground aquifers, from which many northeastern communities draw their drinking water.

Various emissions from coal-burning power plants also produce smog and a wide range of air pollutants that eventually settle to the ground to contaminate the soil. As a result, many of the region's native plants are slowly suffocating in a world of deadly poisons. As the plants disappear, so too do the animals that depend upon them for life.

ENCROACHING CIVILIZATION

Another environmental problem facing the Northeast is urban sprawl. As people move out of towns and cities and into the country, they often end up destroying some of the nation's most environmentally sensitive or agriculturally productive lands. One example is taking place in New York State's Adirondack Park.

"The century-long fight to save Adirondack Park has entered a final, critical stage," warned Charles M. Clusen, executive director of the Adirondack Council, in a recent letter to the *New York Times*. "What is preserved or lost in the next few years will shape the park for all time."

Clusen is particularly concerned about plans by local developers who recently bought several thousand acres of land within the park. The developers told a reporter, "There is no other future for this park than private development, and anybody who doesn't understand that yet is going to learn very quickly."

Situated in scenic upstate New York, Adirondack is the largest park in the contiguous 48 states. Its 6 million acres, constituting about one fifth of the state's size, are a mix of 3.5 million privately owned and 2.5 million publicly owned forest preserve acres. These include some 2,700 lakes and ponds, 5 major river headwaters, 40 peaks more than 4,000 feet in eleva-

Adirondack Park is one of the largest and most important natural preserves in the Northeast.

tion, and 120,000 year-round residents—a number that swells to 220,000 during summer.

Over the years, the state, given the task of acquiring as much of the privately owned lands as possible, has actually acquired very little. The result is that much of the park is now ripe for commercial takeover.

During the early 1970s, developers wanted to build several cities of 10,000 to 12,000 vacation homes each on the park's private lands. Environmentalists stopped the projects by persuading state legislators to enact some of the nation's strictest zoning laws. Their main concern was for the environment. Since the building boom began in the 1970s, lakes George, Placid, and several others have deteriorated in quality to an alarming degree.

FIGHTING BACK

Today, the Adirondack Council is leading the fight to protect the park from wholesale development. The council hopes to persuade the legislature to enact even stricter zoning laws while urging the state to speed up its land-acquisition program in order to better compete with developers. At the same time, the Adirondack Land Trust is devoting half its budget to buying private land within park boundaries.

"If we want to succeed in...permanently protecting the park's lake shores, roadsides, and river corridors," says Clusen, "we have to work fast. We have only a few years left."

Yet as troubling a problem as urban sprawl is for the Northeast, urban waste—the discarded products of an urban society—is even more disturbing.

URBAN WASTE MISMANAGEMENT

Nearly four fifths of all U.S. municipal waste—the garbage we produce in our homes—ends up in landfills. But there are problems with landfilling the Northeast's trash—not the least of which is that its landfill sites are filling up.

In 1978, nearly 20,000 landfills dotted the nation. By 1988, the number had dropped to 6,000. In the past five years alone, 3,000 landfills have closed; by 1993, experts expect some 2,000 more will shut down. America is running out of places to put its trash.[1] And other forms of solid-waste disposal are no more promising.

The Northeast could simply incinerate, or burn, its trash and its problems would be over. Or would they?

Where solid-waste disposal is concerned, out of sight isn't necessarily out of mind. Since both the smoke and the leftover ash from incinerator stacks are harmful to the environment, incineration may not be the best answer to the problem.

THE DANGERS OF INCINERATED WASTE

As household waste is burned, the fly ash it creates settles inside incinerator smokestacks. That ash, one of the most hazardous of all waste materials, according to the Environmental Defense Fund (EDF), contains both cadmium and lead—two highly toxic heavy metals—in concentrations exceeding Environmental Protection Agency (EPA) hazardous-waste-limit standards. Meanwhile, bottom ash, the charred remains of incinerated garbage, has exceeded the EPA's lead limits in four of ten samples taken.

After fly ash is cleaned from smokestacks, it's dumped together with bottom ash in city landfills. There the ash is easily spread by wind and water. As rainwater trickles down through the ash, dioxins (a group of highly toxic chemicals), heavy metals, and other toxic substances go with it. They gradually work their way into streams and underground aquifers and pollute local water supplies. The dioxins and toxic metals leached from the ash accumulate in the food chain and are easily absorbed by various living organisms.[2]

"It's ironic," according to Greenpeace environmentalist Jim Vallette. "The reason cities started building incinerators in the first place is because town dumps were filling up and polluting water supplies. Now they're dumping the same toxics that were in their garbage to start with, plus a whole new set created in the furnaces. The difference is that some of those toxics are more concentrated and more soluble in water than they were in their original state."

The pollutants escaping from incinerator stacks are just as frightening. Besides such highly toxic chemicals as dioxins and carbofurans (chemicals used as insecticides),[3] incinerators emit roughly 27 different metals, over 200 organic chemicals, and a wide range of acidic gases. An average 1,600 ton-a-day incinerator generates .06 pounds of dioxins and carbofurans; 510 pounds of hydrocarbons; 5,000 pounds of lead; 361 pounds of cadmium; 2,244 pounds of chromium; 13,250 pounds of zinc; and 20 pounds of mercury each day.

Of all incinerator-generated chemical pollutants, dioxin is by far the most poisonous. Ironically, most household waste contains few dioxins. The toxins, according to environmental researcher Dr. Barry Commoner, director for the Biology of Natural Systems at Queens College, New York, are actually created inside incinerator smokestacks after burning.

The bottom line is that life in the Northeast is suffering—both wildlife and humans. The EPA estimates that cancer rates in communities located near plants with smokestacks emitting chemical pollutants are two to three times higher than normal. This estimate fails to take into account those toxins that work their way into the food chain.

Yet various technologies exist to limit the release of toxic pollutants such as heavy metals and acidic gases. Even though acid gas scrubbers could reduce the hydrogen chloride emissions of the Peekskill, New York, incinerator from 600 parts per million (ppm) to 10 ppm, few incinerators are so equipped. Several new plants not fitted with scrubbers are believed to be the cause of a pattern of respiratory illness reported in numerous northeastern cities, including Oswego, New York; Windham, Connecticut; and Saugus, Massachusetts.

(opposite page)
Even state-of-the-art incinerators are major polluters of the northeastern environment.

The nation's 100-plus incinerators currently burn about 5 percent of America's garbage, and over 200 additional plants are either planned or currently under construction. By the mid-1990s, as many as 300 incinerators may be burning up to 25 percent of the nation's municipal waste—and emitting five times the pollutants!

"The proposed investment in garbage incineration represents a monumental commitment to a technology which is fast becoming obsolete," according to Dr. Commoner. "If a similar investment were made in setting up and enforcing recycling programs, we would be much closer to solving the solid-waste disposal problem, both ecologically and economically."[4]

A MATTER OF PRIORITIES

Dr. Paul Connet, assistant chemistry professor at St. Lawrence University in Canton, New York, and cofounder of the environmental group, Work on Waste, agrees. "It's a plastic bag crisis, not a waste crisis. The solution is to go down and see what's in our plastic bags. The paper, cardboard, cans, glass, and food are all [recyclable] resources until they're mixed up and put into a plastic bag. Then they're waste. Using high-tech burning machines is simply perfecting the destruction of our natural resources. We need to recycle in a way we've never done before.

One of the most effective means of reducing solid waste is through recycling.

"People are ready for it, but they're not being given the leadership. When given a chance, people recycle. We've got to recycle as if there's a war on. And there is...a war against waste."

Recycling is one of the least expensive means of reducing pollution. Each day, thousands of tons of materials are thrown away by consumers and industry. New York City discards more than 25,000 tons of domestic waste a day. Much of that could be reused, either "as is" or after relatively simple treatment and reprocessing. According to David Morris of the Washington-based Institute for Local Self-Reliance, a city the size of Baltimore disposes of more aluminum than is produced by a small bauxite mine; more copper than a medium-sized copper mine; and more paper than a large stand of timber.

Besides providing a wise approach to resource management, recycling cuts energy consumption and reduces pollution. A Worldwatch Institute study in 1987 found that recycling one aluminum can would save the equivalent of half a can of oil. One ton of reprocessed aluminum eliminates the need for 4 tons of bauxite and more than 1,500 pounds of petroleum coke and pitch while reducing toxic aluminum fluoride from the environment by 77 pounds. Simply doubling the worldwide rate at which aluminum is currently being recycled could eliminate "over a million tons of air pollutants—including toxic fluorides," according to the study. In addition, recycling lowers water use, reduces dependence on foreign oil, and creates jobs and opportunities for small businesses.

Although numerous voluntary recycling programs are popping up in cities throughout the Northeast—in New York, Boston, Washington, and Philadelphia, for example—voluntary programs may not be enough. One such program in Hamburg, New York, met with relative indifference. However, when the town voted to make recycling mandatory, the results were impressive. More than 650 tons of paper, 150 tons of glass, and 110 tons of metal were recycled in the first year, saving taxpayers $24,000 in disposal costs and reducing landfilled trash by 34 percent.[5]

In New York City, where more than 400 million cases of beverages are sold yearly, deposits on recyclable beverage containers have saved the city $50 million to $100 million in energy costs, $50 million in cleanup expenses, and $19 million in household-waste disposal costs in just two years. As a bonus, employment has increased by nearly 4,000 jobs.

In New Jersey, a sign in AT&T's office warns employees, "AT&T's Recycling Program—It's the Law! Virtually all papers are recyclable at AT&T."

The company's policy is a result of New Jersey's mandatory recycling law, but AT&T spokesperson Cheryl La Perna says that the company would recycle its paper even without the law. "Ninety percent of our solid waste is paper. We're a paper factory, no doubt about it."

As a reward for its diligence, the company reported a profit of $190,000 from the collection and sale of 3,800 tons of used office paper during 1988.[6]

THE TOXIC-WASTE PROBLEM

Besides household wastes, the Northeast faces what many environmentalists call the most threatening waste-disposal problem in the world—toxic wastes. These wastes are generated by industry and agriculture and include such potentially deadly substances as chemicals, pesticides, and nuclear waste.

Although estimates of the number of U.S. toxic-waste disposal sites vary, at least 15,000 uncontrolled toxic-waste landfills have been identified, along with 80,000 contaminated surface lagoons. The problem is so widespread that eight out of ten Americans now live near a toxic-waste site, according to the Council on Economic Priorities. Nearly half of all U.S. residents live in counties containing a site classified as among the most dangerous in the United States.

To date, every state except Nevada has identified at least one toxic-waste site for inclusion on the EPA's National Priority List. These sites are all eligible for special cleanup funding under the federal government's emergency Superfund legislation. By 1988, 1,177 such sites had been identified nationwide. Among them, New Jersey listed 110; Pennsylvania, 97; and New York, more than 75.[7]

"The dimensions of controlling toxics are so vast," according to author Jon Naar in his book, *Design for a Livable Planet*, "that even the Environmental Protection Agency finds them almost impossible to comprehend. A ticking time bomb primed to go off is how the agency described the toxic-waste problem."

Toxic Substances Discharged by U.S. Industry, 1987

Destination	Millions of Pounds
Air	2700
Lakes, Rivers and Streams	550
Landfills and Earthen Pits	3900
Treatment and Disposal Facilities	3300
Total	10450

Source: Environmental Protection Agency, reported in *The Washington Post*, April 13, 1989, p. A33

(opposite page)
Even after toxic wastes are sealed and labeled, they often end up back in the environment.

TOXIC-WASTE DISASTER

The EPA was right. In 1979, the New York State commissioner for health finally ordered the evacuation of 240 families from a section in Niagara City called Love Canal. The entire area was cordoned off and the site declared a federal disaster area—the first time in U.S. history that a chemical dumping ground had been so designated.

First excavated in the late 1800s as part of a hydroelectric project planned by the eccentric industrialist William T. Love, Love Canal was used from 1940 to 1952 by the Hooker Chemicals and Plastics Corporation as a dumping ground for its chemical wastes. More than 21,000 tons of waste, much of it carcinogenic, were dumped into the canal.

In 1953, Hooker sold the site to the local board of education for $1. As part of the sales contract, the company was absolved of any future liability from the chemicals in the dump. The board of education soon built a school on the site, and a housing development shortly followed.

Then, in 1977, tests showed that the dump was leaking. The air, soil, and water around the dump site were heavily contaminated by a wide range of toxic and carcinogenic chemicals. Local authorities were slow to take action. That's when the state's health department stepped in and forced the evacuation. In 1980, further studies showed the pollution level to be more extensive than originally thought, and more families were evacuated.[8]

William Sanjour, the chief of the Hazardous Waste Implementation Branch at the time of the Love Canal incident, commented shortly afterward on how the Carter administration had responded to the problem. "The way [the administration] solved their problem was to spend an awful lot of money on the environment but see to it that it didn't do anything. Spending the money satisfied the environmentalists. That's why the Superfund was invented.

"When Love Canal blew up in people's faces and became a very publicized event, the agency's response, I would have thought, would be, 'Well, all right, let's now implement the regulations which will prevent this problem from happening again in the future.'

"They didn't do that. What they did was invent a huge Superfund to clean up the waste instead of preventing it. In other words, if you're faced with an outbreak of polio, what [you're] doing is buying more iron lungs instead of investing in vaccine.... It was a trick. It made the environmentalists think, `Look, we're spending a lot of money in cleaning up waste, so we must be doing something good.'

"It satisfied the waste disposal industry because they made a fortune out of Superfund. What Superfund does is to take waste from one landfill and move it to another landfill. And they [the polluters] get paid for it. In fact, the very same people who Superfund was moving against were in some cases actually getting paid to move the waste around. They pay a small fine for their previous pollution and make a fortune for moving it somewhere else."

The northeastern states are quickly running out of places to landfill their trash.

Meanwhile, the chemical fallout from Love Canal continues. Three other Hooker Chemicals and Plastics Corporation dumps in the area are now known to be leaking. Wastes from one at Hyde Park are oozing directly into the Niagara River, from which nearly 6 million people draw their drinking water. The site contains the largest concentration of dioxin in the world. Another site at Bloody Run Creek, situated across the road from a water-treatment facility serving 100,000 people, is also leaking.

All in all, more than 200 hazardous-waste sites in the Niagara Falls area contain an estimated 8 million tons of waste. And this waste includes more than 1 ton of the deadly toxin, dioxin.

SPREAD OF PCBS

First produced artificially in 1881, polychlorinated biphenyls (PCBs) have been used in various commercial processes since the 1930s. Their high resistance to heat and low electrical conductivity make them valuable compounds in products ranging from fluorescent light bulbs and hydraulic fluid to electrical transformers and capacitors.

Although the toxic effects of PCBs have been known for years, it wasn't until 1968 that the full extent of their dangers were realized when a major pollution incident in Japan resulted in disaster. Shortly after some PCB-contaminated rice oil was consumed there, ten people died. The remaining victims experienced a wide range of symptoms, from loss of hair and discharges from the eyes to jaundice, dizziness, nausea, numbness, darkening of the skin, loss of vision, and various sexual disorders.[9]

A follow-up study showed an unusually high rate of cancer deaths among the more than 1,000 PCB-contaminated victims. Women who had consumed the polluted oil bore children with an exceptionally high rate of birth defects.

Subsequently, Japan banned the use of PCBs in 1972. But no such action took place in the United States, where intense lobbying efforts by the Monsanto Company, the sole manufacturer of PCBs, delayed governmental restrictions against the chemical's use for years.

In a news release issued by E. V. John of the Monsanto Company and dated July 16, 1970, the manufacturer dismissed environmental concerns about PCBs and labeled news stories about the hazards of the chemical's use "sensational."

It wasn't until 1978 that mounting pressure by environmental groups finally persuaded Congress to ban the manufacture of PCBs. But no action was taken to remove products containing PCBs from the marketplace.

Then, in 1981, an explosion in the basement of an office complex in Binghamton, New York, caused an electrical transformer containing PCBs to crack. The intense heat and resulting fire following the explosion caused the PCBs to break down, forming a fine ash contaminated by PCBs, dioxins, and polychlorinated dibenzo-furans (PCBFs), a highly toxic chemical produced when PCBs are exposed to heat.

The polluted ash was carried quickly throughout the building by the air conditioning system. Four years later, the building was still too toxic to enter without protective clothing. Estimates to decontaminate the site in 1985 topped $19 million.

Today, PCB contamination continues to affect nearly every living American. One EPA survey taken prior to the Binghamton disaster found PCBs in virtually all samples of mothers' milk tested—up to ten times the maximum daily limit set by the Food and Drug Administration (FDA). "If human milk were marketed in interstate commerce," wrote author Robert H. Boyle in the book, *Malignant Neglect*, "much of it would be seized and condemned by the FDA."

THE AIR WE BREATHE

The skies over the Northeast are filled with trillions of insects fed upon by thousands of species of birds. The two play a vital link in the food chain and the maintenance of a healthy environment.

But there are changes occurring in these skies—ominous changes that could have long-lasting effects.

Many species of birds most vulnerable to air pollution are disappearing. Meat-, fish-, and carrion-eating birds such as falcons, eagles, hawks, and vultures that live at the top of the food chain are among the first to be affected.

In her sobering account of the state of the environment, author Rachel Carson wrote in *Silent Spring* of the particular susceptibility of birds to such agricultural pesticides as DDT and dieldrin. Likewise, the toxic components of acid rain, which rise from the smokestacks of industry and from the exhausts of automobiles to contaminate every cubic yard of fresh air, eventually fall to Earth to contaminate both surface and groundwater, causing birth defects in nesting water birds.

But birds aren't the only species to succumb to pollution of the skies. In fact, one form of pollution threatens every living, breathing species on Earth.

(opposite page)
These innocent-looking clouds contain destructive acid rain.

ACID RAIN

Acid rain is a serious problem facing northeastern states. When carbon dioxide from coal-burning utility companies scattered across the nation dissolves in moisture in the air, it forms a compound called carbonic acid. As sulfur dioxide, nitrogen oxides, and hydrogen sulfides from burning fossil

U.S. Sources of Carbon Dioxide Emissions

Electric Utilities	33%
Transportation	31%
Industry	24%
Buildings	12%

Source: MacKenzie, *Breathing Easier,* p. 10

fuels are dissolved with carbonic acid, they create sulfuric or nitric acids. These acids settle to the ground with falling rain and dust.

Acid rain damages everything with which it comes in contact—from cars and buildings to lakes, rivers, and streams. It takes a heavy toll on wildlife, as well as on life of a different form—human beings.

"Current levels of acid rain pollution are able to produce substantial adverse health effects in certain segments of the American population, and particularly in children," according to Dr. Philip J. Landrigan, professor of community medicine and pediatrics at the Mt. Sinai School of Medicine in New York City. Landrigan estimates that acid rain is the third largest cause of lung disease behind active cigarette smoking and the passive inhaling of cigarette smoke.[1]

Given the task of providing a "reasonable estimate" of the toll acid rain takes on human health, the Congressional Office of Technology Assessment (OTA) in a report estimated that 50,000 premature deaths a year in the United States and Canada may be linked to sulfates and other particulates in acid rain.

Dr. Richard M. Narkewicz, a Burlington, Vermont, pediatrician, believes that the ingredients of acid rain, particularly ozone, sulfates, and nitrogen oxides, "cause disease in children and aggravate pre-existing respiratory conditions." Prolonged exposure to acid rain could cause chronic lung diseases, such as emphysema and bronchitis.

A number of additional studies over the years have added to the acid-rain-and-health puzzle. Among them:

• Preliminary evidence from the "Harvard Six-City Study" suggests that acid rain and the extremely fine particulates in acid rain produce respiratory diseases in children.

• Carefully controlled studies at New York's University of Rochester showed that exposing normal adults to the kinds of sulfuric-acid aerosols present in acid rain produced "respiratory dysfunction."

• A major New York University study showed how repeated exposures of healthy animals to even "modest" doses of the sulfuric-acid mist contained in acid rain produced "hyperre-sponsive airways." When exposed to air pollution or cold air, the animals contracted "bronchoconstriction similar to that seen in asthma."

ALL SMOGGED IN

Smog (mostly ozone and peroxyacetyl nitrate—PAN—created by the action of sunlight on various emissions from automobile exhausts and industrial smokestacks) has long been an unwelcome guest in such northeastern cities as New York, Philadelphia, and Washington, D.C. But recent studies show it's now appearing in record proportions in suburban and rural America as well. For the first time since measurements began, excessive ozone levels were recently recorded in rural Maine and northern New York State. Unless steps are taken to stop smog soon, the problem is expected to grow.

A POSSIBLE SOLUTION

Scientists in New Haven, Connecticut, have concluded that, over the course of a single growing season, a large sugar maple tree can remove as much airborne lead as that produced by burning a thousand gallons of gasoline. An acre of mature sycamore trees could capture 15 tons of pollutants; an acre of elms or beech, 20 tons a year.

Urban planners are beginning to respond to such findings. In many cities throughout the Northeast, there's a growing appreciation of trees as natural cleansers of our air. But trees aren't a cure for a polluted environment. Many have difficulty themselves surviving life in the city. But some varieties of trees in some locations are beginning to make a difference.

But which trees? And in which locations? Those are not always easy questions for scientists to answer. Too much ozone in the environment destroys the tiny stomata on the trees' leaves. Steady exposure to toxic substances in the air may kill some trees. Throughout New England and the Appalachians, toxic air pollution and acid rain are destroying forests located miles from urban centers. Then, too, the pollutants absorbed by some leaves may eventually re-enter the atmosphere when the leaves are collected and incinerated in the fall.

But red maples, white birch, and sweet gum trees actually seem to thrive on sulfur dioxide—one of the main ingredients of industrial pollution—converting it to harmless substances in the process. White oaks are especially adept at absorbing ozone, a major component of smog. And the needles of most pine trees effectively filter out airborne dust and particulates all year long.

Trees such as these soft maples make excellent natural air cleansers.

"Trees display a very large surface area to the air," according to William H. Smith, a forest scientist at Yale University. "It's clear that they can remove a lot of material, but the capability varies greatly, depending on the species of the tree, its size, health, and the time of year."

However, the pollution rates in some cities are so great that it would take huge stands of trees to begin cleaning up the air.

"Individual trees—even one or two or three rows planted along a street or highway—are not going to help much," Smith says. "But if we could design an urban environment from scratch, it would probably be very useful to incorporate large bands of green space."

Scientists estimate that each maple, oak, or linden tree has the capacity to remove three-quarters of a ton of dust and soot a year from city air. At that rate, nearly 473 square miles of forest would be required to clean the air of a city the size of Pittsburgh—an area approximately eight times as large as the city itself.

Obviously, trees are not the only answer to urban air pollution. But trees in combination with decreasing pollution emissions in the Northeast's most populous cities may play an important role in safeguarding America's atmosphere in the future.

INDOOR AIR POLLUTION

Although smog and acid rain end up grabbing most of the local newspaper headlines, a very different type of air pollution is slowly stealing life from those who come in contact with it. Often referred to as indoor air pollution, it too is a killer.

Indoor air pollution comes from many different sources—bacteria, mold, mildew, and animal dander; carbon monoxide from leaking chimneys and furnaces, wood stoves and fireplaces, tobacco smoke, and automobile exhausts from attached garages; asbestos from old or damaged insulation, fireproofing, and acoustical tiles; formaldehyde from plywood, wall paneling, foam insulation, and cigarette tobacco smoke; lead from automobile exhausts, sanding or burning lead paint, and soldering; nitrogen dioxide from kerosene heaters, unvented gas stoves and heaters, and tobacco smoke; organic gases from paint, paint solvents, wood preservatives, aerosol sprays, cleansers and disinfectants, moth repellents, air fresheners, stored fuels, and dry-cleaned clothing; particulates from fireplaces and wood stoves, kerosene heaters, and tobacco smoke; pesticides including household sprays and lawn-and-garden products; and others.[2]

The EPA estimates that as many as one fifth to one third of all office buildings and homes in the United States currently suffer from polluted indoor air. That pollution may come from the building itself, the chemicals used within it, the activities of its inhabitants, or even the ground on which the building sits.

CLOSET RADIOACTIVITY

One of the deadliest forms of indoor air pollution is radon, a colorless, odorless, tasteless radioactive gas. It's generated by the natural decay of uranium in the soil and is usually concentrated in the basements or crawl spaces of houses, especially in newer, air-tight, energy-efficient buildings.

In December 1985, Stanley Watras, an engineer entering the Limerick Nuclear Power Plant in Pottstown, Pennsylvania, set off a radioactive screening device even before the plant was fully operational. An investigation revealed the source to be an alarmingly high level of radon in Watras' body. The radon came from the family's home, which was built above an area of high radon concentration—a frequent occurrence in parts of Pennsylvania, New Jersey, and New York.

In 1988, the EPA's State Radon Survey found that nearly one in three houses contained radon levels above the measurement at which the EPA recommends action to reduce the hazardous gas. As many as 10 million homes are currently suspected of emitting hazardous concentrations of radon throughout the United States, a majority of them in the Northeast.

"Radon-inducing lung cancer is one of today's most serious public health issues," according to Dr. Vernon Houk, assistant surgeon general of the Public Health Service. The EPA estimates that approximately 5,000 to 20,000 lung cancer deaths a year in the United States result from radon, which is particularly harmful to smokers.

Fortunately, the gas can be detected by simple do-it-yourself test kits sold in hardware stores and home centers across the nation. For those houses showing high levels of radon, various moderately priced radon-proofing procedures are available. For information on radon-testing procedures, call 1-800-SOS-RADON toll free.

(opposite page)
Although many forms of outdoor air pollution are obvious, indoor pollution is less visible.

THREE MILE ISLAND

Although radon is a persistent source of radioactive pollution, it's not the cause of all radioactivity. In the early morning stillness of March 28, 1979, several dozen workers reported as usual to the Three Mile Island nuclear power plant near Harrisburg, Pennsylvania. Soon after, trouble struck. One of two pressurized water reactors closed down just seconds after a water-coolant pump failed to work. Although the reactor had closed, heat from the radioactive energy inside the core caused internal temperatures to rise sharply.

To make matters worse, a relief valve that opened in the first few seconds of the accident failed to close, although indicators in the control room showed that it had. The open valve bled off most of what little coolant remained in the core.

When the emergency core-cooling system opened, operators mistakenly closed it. The increasing temperatures in the core caused steam bubbles to form in the coolant, speeding up the rate of water loss. Within two hours, the water level in the reactor had dropped below the top of the radioactive fuel rods, forcing temperatures even higher. The metal casing around the fuel rods melted and reacted with the remaining water to form hydrogen gas. Videotapes of the incident later showed that the uranium itself may have started to melt.

Soon the remaining coolant pumps began shaking violently. The operators once again mistakenly closed them. By the time reactor manufacturer employees arrived and flooded the reactor, bringing internal temperatures back down to normal, the reactor had suffered a hydrogen explosion.

Although little radioactivity was actually released into the environment at the time of the accident, the reactor itself remained highly contaminated. Nearly a year after the accident, 57 curies of highly radioactive Krypton-85 were still trapped inside the reactor dome. Authorities finally decided to release the gas by venting it into the atmosphere, despite public protests.

When the level of radiation inside the plant finally dropped to a level safe enough for a work crew in radiation suits to enter, they found a completely collapsed core. By 1987, the plant's owners, General Public Utilities, decided that the only

way to contain the mess was to remove as much contaminated material as possible and then entomb the reactor in concrete.

The incident at Pennsylvania's Three Mile Island nuclear power plant nearly ended in catastrophe.

Luckily, the containment system of the reactor at Three Mile Island had managed to hold in an estimated 18 billion curies of radioactivity. Had the containment system failed, the plant would have released nearly 100 times the amount of radioactivity released in the Soviet catastrophe at Chernobyl. The incident at Three Mile Island was America's closest brush with nuclear catastrophe. It offered support to environmentalists who argued that nuclear reactors pose more of a threat to the environment than they're worth. By 1989, Three Mile Island cleanup costs had topped $1 billion and were still rising.

Today, more than a decade later, serious questions remain about the use of nuclear energy, as well as about the safe disposal of nuclear wastes generated from nuclear power plants. Some of these remain highly radioactive and dangerous to all life-forms for up to half a million years—longer by far than Homo sapiens has walked the Earth!

THE WATER WE DRINK

Eons ago, life on Earth began in the seas. Today, water remains the common thread that binds all life. But the waterways that once provided food, transportation, and recreation for native American Indians and, later, European settlers are in trouble. Toxic waste, agricultural runoff, eutrophication, oil spills—all are turning once clean, natural sources of fresh water into cesspools of pollution. Even the mighty Atlantic Ocean has become little more than a massive dump for cities up and down the Atlantic coast. And the pollution continues.

- New York State officials currently warn residents to limit consumption of fish from the Hudson River and nearby coastal waters to one serving a week in order to avoid ingesting too many toxic pollutants.

- Illnesses such as cholera, hepatitis, and gastroenteritis from eating seafood containing toxic heavy metals are increasing.

- Aquatic plants and marine life are slowly strangling on chemical fallout from the nation's most persistent polluters.

ACID RAIN'S EFFECT ON WATERWAYS

Although acid rain begins as an air pollutant, it soon falls to the ground to pollute the Northeast's fragile waterways. To draw attention to the severity of the problem, the National Wildlife Federation published in 1989 a state-by-state list of 1,700 lakes with acidity levels too high to support life.

The list, based on EPA tests of a fraction of the large lakes in various regions of the country, represents only "the tip of the

(opposite page)
Much of the water on which people in the Northeast rely is already dangerously polluted.

iceberg," according to the federation. The EPA conservatively estimates that another 14,000 lakes—as many as one fifth of those in Massachusetts, New Hampshire, New York, and Rhode Island—are well on their way to destruction.

The problem is most serious in the Northeast. This is because acid rain from automobile exhausts and industrial smokestacks in the North Central region and Ohio River valley blows eastward on prevailing winds. Coal-fired power plants also contribute to the problem, adding about 20 million tons of sulfur dioxide—a main ingredient in acid rain—to the atmosphere each year. If the damaging effects of acid rain are to be reduced, so must the sulfur dioxide.

On June 12, 1989, President George Bush called for a reduction of 10 million tons of sulfur dioxide by the year 2000, with half that reduction taking place by 1995. Reaching such an ambitious goal will require switching to low-sulfur coal or oil as a fuel. Shifting to natural gas is even more effective, since gas contains almost no sulfur. But that would require the installation of expensive new furnaces.

The president's goal also calls for lowering the quantity of atmospheric nitrogen oxides, another major ingredient in acid rain. That will require new technologies and alternate sources of energy such as solar power. It also means the overall reduction of automobile emissions, either by installing more efficient catalytic converters or by using alternate fuels.

Although the costs are expected to be enormous, the harm to the environment in not taking action is even greater.

OIL SPILLS AND THE LOSS OF WILDLIFE

The devastating effects of the Alaskan Exxon *Valdez* oil spill were still being talked about when tragedy struck the Northeast. Within a 12-hour period in June 1989, two oil tankers dumped hundreds of thousands of gallons of oil in the Delaware River and Rhode Island's Narragansett Bay. As the oil washed ashore, it formed a thick, tarlike skin, destroying the feeding and breeding habitats of countless species of wildlife. Although the cleanup operations were more successful than those in the Alaskan spill, thousands of animals along the northeastern coast perished.

But accidents involving ships at sea and offshore oil rigs actually account for less than a third of all coastal oil spills. Far more oil pollution occurs as a result of municipal and industrial runoff and the periodic cleaning of ships' bilges and tanks at sea. Although such activities are illegal, catching ships in the act of dumping oil has proved nearly impossible.[1]

WASTEWATER POLLUTANTS

Wastewater from human sewage is another form of pollution plaguing the Northeast. Water contaminated with high levels of bacteria deplete the oxygen, killing off numerous forms of aquatic life. Once all the oxygen is consumed, anaerobic bacteria—those that require no oxygen for survival—begin to multiply, destroying any remaining aquatic life.

Yet numerous municipalities still channel raw sewage into the nearest waterway. It's the easiest and least expensive means of disposing of the waste. As a result, commercial fishing has suffered, and numerous beaches have been closed to swimming and other activities throughout the Northeast.

"NO SWIMMING ALLOWED!"

As newspaper headlines in the late 1980s screamed of human excrement washing up onto previously clean sands, people became angry. The culprit wasn't one or two polluters but scores of them. Rainstorms overpowered the city gutters of Manhattan and Newark and sent their contents funneling toward the sea. Waste-treatment plants overwhelmed by sewage released untreated human excrement into open waters. Oceangoing ships regularly dumped their wastes in the sea.

Although the Clean Water Act of 1972 bans the discharge of any sewage until 85 percent of the bacteria and pollutants are removed, 34 northeastern cities were doing little more than screening out large floating debris as of July 1, 1988, the deadline for compliance with the act. Meanwhile, barges carrying treated sewage and garbage continued dumping their loads. That, too, was illegal as of 1981. But New York State won a court-ordered extension on complying with the law until it could find a reasonable alternative to its problems.

Pollutants dumped into the oceans regularly wash ashore, fouling beaches and destroying wildlife.

Shortly after the dumping site off New Jersey's coastline had become too polluted to support marine life, the barges were ordered to begin using a new site on the edge of the continental shelf.[2] The new area currently receives more than 5 million gallons of sewage and sludge a day. Not surprisingly, commercial fishermen have reported decreased catches and more diseased lobsters and crabs.

Realizing it would eventually have to clean up its act, New Jersey passed legislation aimed at ending its dumping practices by 1991. Meanwhile, Congress moved toward banning all dumping by the early 1990s. But New York and New Jersey are still hauling their municipal wastes to sea, and neither state has yet found an acceptable alternative to the problem.

After trash, medical garbage, and bacteria closed beaches along the East Coast in 1988, New Jersey launched a massive promotional campaign, promising that "the only thing on our beaches this summer [in 1989] will be people."

But high bacteria counts from raw sewage and floating trash as contaminated medical syringes closed 13 Cape May County and all Ocean City beaches in July. Similar pollution crises were reported up and down the Atlantic seaboard.

SAVING THE CHESAPEAKE

Chesapeake Bay has long been one of the greatest producers of seafood on the North Atlantic coast. But in recent years, its yields of crabs, oysters, striped bass, cod, and other high quality foods have fallen because of water pollution. The pollution comes not only from oil spills, toxic chemicals, and sewage, but also from industrial wastes, acid rain, and agricultural chemicals.[3]

Today, the bay contains a thick growth of algae that's using up the water's vital supply of dissolved oxygen. A 1983 EPA report pinpointed the main source of algal growth as agricultural fertilizers. The fertilizers come from the manure from livestock in the Susquehanna River valley above the bay. Yet valley farmers supplement the nitrogen-rich manure with an average of $2,200 a year worth of chemical fertilizers such as anhydrous ammonia—much of which runs off farmers' fields and into the rivers feeding the bay.

FERTILIZERS RUN TO SEA

A recent program called the Chesapeake Bay Water Quality Project studied the relationship between fertilizers and their effect on water pollution in the area. Researchers have concluded that farmers who grow their own feed crops apply twice as much commercial fertilizer to their soils as necessary. The result is that millions of dollars' worth of commercial nitrogen runs off the soil and into underground reservoirs connected to the Susquehanna River.

When dairy farmer Paul Clugston joined the Chesapeake Bay Water Quality Project in 1985, he'd been spending thousands of dollars a year on fertilizers he didn't actually need. At the suggestion of project researchers, Clugston built a pit to store and compost the manure from his cows for use on his 300 acres of land. That manure now provides half the fertilizer he uses and saves Clugston $4,000 a year.[4]

Unfortunately, such agricultural reforms are few and far between. Still missing from the crusade to save the Chesapeake, along with the Northeast's other valuable waterways, are laws designed to prevent the pollution. Until they're passed, the environment will continue to suffer.

A TIME FOR ACTION

Throughout the Northeast, the endangered animal list reads like a *Who's Who* from the past: the Indiana bat, southern bald eagle, Eastern cougar, Maryland darter, Delmarva Peninsula fox squirrel, Eskimo curlew (one of the rarest birds on Earth), longjaw cisco, blue pike, gray wolf, Plymouth red-bellied turtle, and shortnose sturgeon.

In addition, nearly 8 percent of all plant species are endangered, according to the Center for Plant Conservation. As many as 700 more may become extinct by the year 2000.

But someone is listening. During the last century and a half, environmentalists such as John Muir, Henry David Thoreau, and Aldo Leopold spoke out in favor of a clean, healthy, pollution-free America. More recently, people such as Dr. Barry Commoner, Jacques Cousteau, and Ralph Nader have lobbied for greater governmental support of anti-pollution laws—laws designed to help save not only the environmentally sensitive region of the northeastern United States, but also the rest of the world, to which America's Northeast is tightly linked.

Joining them in their battle have been hundreds of thousands of heroes in the day-to-day battle for Earth's survival.

(opposite page)
The red wolf is just one of the animals quickly disappearing from the woods and forests of the Northeast.

REUSING WASTE

One of the Northeast's most successful waste-recovery facilities is located in Wellesley, Massachusetts, a suburban residential community 25 minutes from Boston. Referred to locally as "the dump," the center is situated around an obsolete incinerator. Its neatly mowed grass, gently curving driveway, and picnic tables make it look more like a park than a garbage dump.

Although Wellesley doesn't have a regular trash-collection program, more than 85 percent of its residents take their own trash to the dump. Next to various drop-off containers for recyclable materials is a Goodwill Industries trailer that accepts small appliances and used clothing. In the basement of the old incinerator is a special area for car batteries, tires, and waste oil. Behind the building is a giant compost bin where residents take their grass clippings and other organic waste and pick up last year's compost for use on their lawns and gardens.

The Wellesley center also has a swap shop where residents can exchange anything from magazines and corkscrews to discarded furniture and appliances. Commercial haulers can buy metal, paper, cardboard, and other recyclable materials.

In 1987, more than 16 percent of the nearly 18,000 tons of waste processed at the center was recycled. In 1988, that figure rose to 24 percent. The results netted Wellesley $186,000, mostly from the sale of recyclables, as well as from transportation and landfilling savings. A similar center in Wilton, New Hampshire, has had even better success with a 45 percent recycling rate.[1]

BATTLE OF THE MOHAWK

Ruth Caplan, executive director of Environmental Action, decided to join the celebration on Earth Day in 1970. Like others in her upstate New York community, she walked the shore of Lake Ontario picking up bottles and cans. Intrigued by the success of the grass-roots effort, she subscribed to *Environmental Action* magazine.

Nearly a year later, Caplan joined with some friends to discuss the deteriorating condition of the environment. Soon, the neighborhood group grew into a larger, more dedicated organization. From that group, Ecology Action of Oswego was born.

One day, a strawberry farmer showed up at a meeting. He had with him a tape recorder, and he played a tape about radioactive plutonium. When the tape was finished, the farmer told the group that his farm was next to a nuclear power plant that Niagara Mohawk, an upstate New York

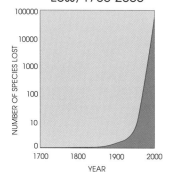

Estimated Annual Rate of Species Loss, 1700-2000

Source: Based on estimates in Norman Myers (ed., *Gaia: An Atlas of Planet Management* (Garden City, NY: Anchor Books, 1984), p. 155

power utility, had put into operation in 1969 at Nine Mile Point. He said that the New York State Power Authority was building another plant just nine miles from the center of town.

With each successive meeting, the environmental group learned more about nuclear power. The more they learned, the more they realized they didn't want nuclear waste leaking from storage tanks in their neighborhood the way it had in Hanford, Washington; West Valley, New York; and Maxey Flats, Kentucky.

"Then a public notice appeared in our local newspaper," says Caplan. "The U.S. Atomic Energy Commission notified us that the Power Authority wanted permission to operate the reactor they had been building. Then a second notice appeared...Niagara Mohawk wanted permission to construct a third nuclear plant at Nine Mile Point."

The day of reckoning had arrived. The group met to plan a response to the notices. Nearly half decided it was time for action. "It felt like my first jump off a diving board," says Caplan, "scary, but exhilarating."

The group hired a lawyer to represent them. They tracked down expert witnesses. They sold tacos at the town fair to finance their efforts.

The group failed to stop the construction of the reactors. But what they learned taught them how to bring a case before the Atomic Energy Commission (AEC). When another utility announced plans to build another nuclear plant with four other utility companies, the group was prepared to spring into action.

"We found support from environmental and peace groups in nearby cities—Ithaca, Rochester, and Syracuse," says Caplan. "And we discovered that farmers didn't want the high-voltage transmission lines running across their land, lines that would have to be built to bring the electricity from the nuclear plant."

Together, the groups formed the Lakeshore Alliance and sent out a united message: "No More Nukes!" Together, they organized, petitioned, and won. Standing toe-to-toe against utility company lawyers who had earned more than $5 million in fees, the alliance won. In the end, the state siting board reversed its approval for the plant.

"The fact that so many people were involved convinced the siting board to reconsider its decision," says Caplan. "The marches, rallies, and TV coverage hadn't gone unnoticed. We won because people in upstate New York had begun to take conservation seriously. The organizing, individual actions, and legal strategies added up to the final victory."[2]

A POLITICAL VICTORY

Every 10 years, environmentally concerned citizens gather to celebrate Earth Day.

In 1983, EPA attempts to investigate toxic-waste sites in Philadelphia resulted in numerous violent incidents in which federal agents were attacked by dogs, state inspectors were shot at, and one environmental inspector was badly beaten. Similar incidents occurred across the country. The reason, according to author David Day in his book, *The Environmental Wars*, was general political apathy toward the environment.

When President Jimmy Carter opened the 1980 Earth Day celebrations, he emphasized that the battle to save the environment had only begun. Carter, along with Gerald Ford and Richard M. Nixon before him, had put increasing pressure on environmental polluters to clean up their act. The EPA, long understaffed and poorly funded, had become a billion-dollar watchdog agency.

Sadly, when Ronald Reagan took office, his administration ignored nearly all matters related to the environment. Environmentalists viewed the Reagan administration's efforts as regressive and even corrupt. Under Reagan, the EPA and the Department of the Interior were packed with "industrial lobbyists and lawyers whose chief function seemed to be to dismantle environmental legislation or to make it ineffective," according to Day.

"Evidence of extreme conflicts of interest and manipulation of funds led to what many journalists dubbed the `Sewergate Scandal,' which resulted in the resignation of EPA head Ann Burford, whom Reagan had appointed." But the greatest setback for Reagan's anti-environmentalists was the forced resignation of the powerful head of the Department of the Interior, James Watt.

Environmentalists applauded the resignations. Even the conservative *New York Times* viewed the resignations as "the coming-of-age of the environmental movement."

The ability of the environmental movement to create public awareness and effectively use its legal and political clout was the dawn of a new era for the Northeast. It was a new era for the rest of America, too—an era long overdue and desperately needed.

WHAT WE CAN DO

The American Northeast has serious environmental problems. Its landfills are seeping toxic wastes; its waters are rife with sewage and heavy metals; its air is fouled with acid rain.

These are the diseases of a thoughtless society, but we can take steps to cure them.

No one person can follow all of these suggestions. But everyone should try to follow as many as possible. In the process, we'll take a giant step toward cleaning up the Northeast and saving the environment from ecological disaster.

FOR THE LAND

- Inquire about hazardous-waste production and disposal in your community.

- Identify local industries that create hazardous wastes and learn about their disposal procedures.

- Contact national organizations active on the issue of hazardous waste and subscribe to newsletters to keep up to date on recent developments and legislation.

- Form a consumer group with neighbors or classmates and buy pesticide-free organic foods in bulk from local stores. Ask grocery stores and supermarket chains to carry produce free of toxic chemicals.

- Dispose of hazardous household compounds safely.

- Take used motor oil and antifreeze to a gas station with an oil-recycling program.

- Eliminate the use of pesticides on your garden and lawn.

(opposite page)
People of all ages can become active in neighborhood recycling programs.

- Contact local authorities about recycling programs. If none is available, start one!

- Contact neighboring recycling groups, private recyclers, and national recycling organizations. For information about recycling plastics, call 1-800-542-7780 toll free.

- Organize neighbors or classmates in roadside walks to collect cans, bottles, and other recyclable trash.

- Organize community pickups of recyclable materials.

- Reduce the amount of nonrecyclable materials you buy and use.

- Start a petition for the appointment of a full-time recycling coordinator in your state and local community.

FOR THE WATER

- If you live in a coastal area, become active in local groups concerned with coastal issues. Learn about current needs, laws, and problems related to coastal issues.

- Work with local fishermen and boaters on the problems associated with dumping solid wastes into the ocean.

- Support efforts to protect those remaining undeveloped coastlines from future development.

- Encourage plans to set up marine reserves in which future development is restricted or prohibited.

- Work for the stricter regulation of human-waste disposal and more efficient, alternative uses for these wastes.

- Attend meetings concerned with such coastal issues as waste disposal in the ocean; the building of new industrial and power plants; wetlands protection; oil, gas, and mineral reserve development; and the prevention and cleanup of accidental oil spills and discharges.

- Use nonpolluting phosphate-free detergents or soap flakes.

- Dispose of unwanted hazardous chemicals such as pesticides and cleaning compounds in approved sanitary landfills and take advantage of approved community collection points.

- Conserve water use in your home and on your property.

- If your house uses a septic waste-disposal system, make sure your parents keep it properly maintained.

- Suggest to your local public-works department the use of porous asphalt or modular paving materials to reduce runoff from rainfall.

IN GENERAL

- Volunteer for service in organizations active in preventing air pollution or in monitoring and enforcing air-quality standards.

- Join organizations and subscribe to newsletters to keep you up to date on the latest developments in clean-air legislation.

- Conserve energy however possible, thus reducing the need for fossil fuels that contribute to the problems of acid rain.

- Plant as many trees as possible, especially around your town. Not only will they absorb carbon dioxide and give off oxygen, but also they'll cool the buildings in summer, thus reducing the need for air conditioning.

- Write public-service announcements for local radio and television stations (especially local-access cable channels) and write letters to the editor of local newspapers on the subject of environmental protection.

- Find out if schools, colleges, and libraries in your area have courses and programs relating to acid rain. If not, suggest that they start them.

FOR MORE INFORMATION

The following toll-free hot-line telephone numbers provide information ranging from pesticide use to asbestos in homes; from hazardous-waste disposal to chemical-emergency preparedness.

- Asbestos Hotline (1-800-334-8571). Provides information on asbestos and asbestos abatement programs; Mon. to Fri., 8:15 a.m. to 5 p.m.

- Chemical Emergency Preparedness Program Hotline (1-800-535-0202). For information on community preparedness for chemical accidents, etc.; Mon. to Fri., 8:30 a.m. to 4:30 p.m.

- Inspector General's Whistle Blower Hotline (1-800-424-4000). For confidential reporting of EPA-related waste, fraud, abuse, or mismanagement; Mon. to Fri., 10 a.m. to 3 p.m.

- National Pesticides Telecommunications Network Hotline (1-800-858-7378). Provides information about pesticides, toxicity, management, health and environmental effects, safety practices, and cleanup and disposal; 7 days, 24 hours a day.

- National Response Center Hotline (1-800-424-8802). For reporting oil and hazardous chemical spills; 7 days, 24 hours a day.

- Superfund Hotline (1-800-424-9346). Provides Superfund information and technical assistance; Mon. to Fri., 8:30 a.m. to 4:30 p.m.

The following list includes organizations that can provide information and materials on various topics of environmental concern in the Northeast.

American Rivers
 Conservation Council
801 Pennsylvania Ave.
 SE
Washington, D.C. 20003
202-547-6900

AmericanWater
 Resources Association
5410 Grosvenor Lane
Bethesda, MD 20814
301-492-8600

Center for Clean Air
 Policy
444 N. Capitol St.
Washington, D.C. 20001
202-624-7709

Center for Marine
 Conservation
1725 DeSales St. NW
Washington, D.C. 20036
202-429-5609

Citizens for Ocean Law
1601 Connecticut Ave.
 NW
Washington, D.C. 20009
202-462-3737

Coastal Program
 Manager
Div. of Local
 Government and
 Community Services
Dept. of State
162 Washington St.
Albany, NY 12231
518-474-3643

Common Cause
2030 M St. NW
Washington, D.C. 20036
202-833-1200

Council for Solid Waste
 Solutions
1275 K St. NW
Washington, D.C. 20005
202-371-5319

Council on
 Environmental Quality
722 Jackson Place NW
Washington, D.C. 20006
202-395-5750

Defenders of Wildlife
1244 19th St. NW
Washington, D.C. 20036
202-659-9510

Dept. of Environmental
 Conservation
50 Wolf Rd.
Albany, NY 12233
518-457-5400

Department of
 Environmental
 Management
9 Hayes St.
Providence, RI 02908
401-277-3429

Division of Coastal
 Resources
Dept. of Environmental
 Protection
CN 401, Trenton, NJ
 08635
609-292-2795

Environmental Action
1525 New Hampshire
 Ave. NW
Washington, D.C. 20036
202-745-4870

Environmental Coalition
 for North America
1325 G St. NW
Washington, D.C. 20005
202-289-5009

Environmental Defense
 Fund
275 Park Ave. S.
New York, NY 10010
212-505-2100

Friends of the Earth
530 7th St. SE
Washington, D.C. 20003
202-543-4312

Greenpeace USA
1436 U St. NW
Washington, D.C. 20009
202-462-1177

Izaak Walton League
1701 N. Ft. Myer Dr.
Arlington, VA 22209
703-528-1818

Keep America Beautiful,
 Inc.
Mill River Plaza
9 W. Broad St.
Stamford, CT 06902
(Phone # unavailable)

National Association for
 Plastic Container
 Recovery
5024 Parkway Plaza
 Blvd.
Charlotte, NC 28217
704-357-3250

National Audubon
 Society
833 Third Ave.
New York, NY 10022
212-832-3200

National Clean Air
 Coalition
801 Pennsylvania Ave.
 SE
Washington, D.C. 20003
202-543-8200

National Coalition
 against the Misuse of
 Pesticides
530 7th St. SE
Washington, D.C. 20001
202-543-5450

National Coalition for
 Marine Conservation
1 Post Office Square
Boston, MA 02109
617-338-2909

National Geographic
 Society
17th and M Streets NW
Washington, D.C. 20036
202-857-7000

National Recycling
 Coalition
45 Rockefeller Plaza,
 Room 2350
New York, NY 10111
212-765-1800

National Wildlife
 Federation
1412 16th St. NW
Washington, D.C. 20036
202-737-2024

The Nature Conservancy
1815 N. Lynn St.
Arlington, VA 22209
703-841-4860

The Oceanic Society
1536 16th St. NW
Washington, D.C. 20036
(Phone # unavailable)

Sierra Club
530 Bush St.
San Francisco, CA 94108
415-981-8634

United Nations
 Environment Program
2 U.N. Plaza
New York, NY 10022
212-963-8139

U.S. Dept. of Agriculture
Independence Ave.
 between 12th and 14th
 Streets SW
Washington, D.C. 20250
202-477-8732

U.S. Environmental
 Protection Agency
401 M St. SW
Washington, D.C. 20460
202-541-4040

U.S. Fish and Wildlife
 Service
Dept. of the Interior
Washington, D.C. 20240
202-343-1100

U.S. Forest Service
P.O. Box 96090
Washington, D.C. 20090
202-447-3957

Wilderness Society
1400 Eye St. NW
Washington, D.C. 20005
202-842-3400

Worldwatch Institute
1776 Massachusetts Ave.
 NW
Washington, D.C. 20036
202-452-1999

World Wildlife Fund
1250 24th St. NW
Washington, D.C. 20037
202-293-4800

— N O T E S —

INTRODUCTION

1. David Rains Wallace, *Life in the Balance* (New York: Harcourt Brace Jovanovich, Publishers, 1987), p. 71.
2. Ibid, pp. 70 - 72.
3. Ibid, pp. 72 - 73.

CHAPTER ONE: THE LAND WE WALK

1. *The Global Ecology Handbook* (Boston: Beacon Press, 1990), p. 276.
2. Ibid, pp. 275 - 276.
3. *The Universal Almanac* (Kansas City, MO: Universal Press Syndicate Company, 1989), pp. 376 - 377.
4. Jon Naar, *Design for a Livable Planet* (New York: Harper & Row, 1990), p. 13.
5. Ibid, p. 19.
6. Lyndon Stambler, "Reach Out and Recycle Something," *Sierra*, Nov./Dec., 1989, p. 23.
7. *The Global Ecology Handbook*, p. 248.
8. David Day, *The Environmental Wars* (New York: St. Martin's Press, 1989), pp. 199 - 201.
9. Naar, *Design for a Livable Planet*, p. 45.

CHAPTER TWO: THE AIR WE BREATHE

1. Ruth Caplan, *Our Earth, Ourselves* (New York: Bantam Books, 1990), p. 92.
2. *The Universal Almanac*, pp. 374 - 375.

CHAPTER THREE: THE WATER WE DRINK

1. Ibid, p. 372.
2. David K. Bulloch, *The Wasted Ocean* (New York: Lyons & Burford, 1989), p. 63.
3. Ibid, 52.
4. Wallace, *Life in the Balance*, p. 259.

CHAPTER FOUR: A TIME FOR ACTION

1. Naar, *Design for a Livable Planet*, p. 16.
2. Caplan, *Our Earth, Ourselves*, pp. 259 - 263.

GLOSSARY

Acid rain. Rain containing a high concentration of acids from various pollutants such as sulfur dioxide, nitrogen oxide, etc.

Air pollution. The transfer of contaminating substances into the atmosphere, usually as a result of human activities.

Algae. Primitive green plants, many of which are microscopic.

Aquifer. Water-bearing rock or soil.

Atmosphere. A mass of gases surrounding the Earth.

Carcinogen. A substance known to cause cancer.

Compost. A fertilizer made up of organic materials.

Compound. A substance with fixed composition and containing more than one element.

Dioxins. A group of extremely hazardous chemicals known to be carcinogenic.

Ecology. The branch of science concerned with the interrelationship of organisms and their environment.

Ecosystem. A functioning unit of the environment that includes all living organisms and physical features within a given area.

Energy. The ability to perform work.

Erosion. The removal and transportation of soil by wind, running water, or glaciation.

Eutrophication. A natural process in which lakes gradually become too productive, often due to the introduction of growth-stimulating materials such as phosphates.

Fertilizer. A substance used to make soil more productive.

Fly ash. The often highly toxic soot and ash that accumulate on the inside of incinerator plant smokestacks.

Fossil fuels. Various fuel materials such as coal, oil, and natural gas created from the remains of once-living organisms.

Glacier. A large body of ice moving slowly down a slope or spreading outward on a land surface.

Groundwater. Water that is contained in subsurface rock and soil formations.

Hazardous waste. The extremely dangerous by-product of civilization that, by its chemical makeup, is harmful to life.

Heavy metal. A metal such as mercury or lead that is harmful to life.

Homo erectus. Scientific name for one of humankind's ancestral species.

Homo sapiens. Scientific name for modern humans.

Incinerator. A massive furnace used for burning waste.

Insecticide. Any of a wide range of chemicals designed to kill insects.

Irrigation. The process of diverting water from its source to farmland in order to increase crop yields.

Landfill. A site for the disposal of garbage and other waste products.

Leaching. The dissolving and transporting of materials by water seeping downward through soil.

Nuclear energy. Energy from the nucleus of an atom.

Nuclear waste. The long-lived, extremely dangerous by-product of nuclear energy or nuclear weapons production.

Organic farming. The process of farming without the use of environmentally dangerous chemicals in the form of fertilizers or pesticides.

Ozone. A naturally present gas in the atmosphere; also, an artificially produced gas that is a major ingredient in smog.

Particulates. Extremely small bits of dust, soot, soil, etc., that may become airborne.

PCBs. A group of highly toxic organic compounds once widely used as liquid coolants and insulators in industrial equipment.

Pesticide. A general term for any of a large number of chemical compounds used to kill pests such as insects, weeds, fungi, bacteria, etc.

Pollution. A general term for environmental contaminants.

Power. The rate at which work can be performed.

Radon. A naturally occurring radioactive gas that in high concentrations is harmful to organisms.

Recycling. The recovery and reuse of material resources.

Runoff. Water that moves across the surface of the land faster than the soil can absorb it.

Scrubbing. The removal of pollutants from a stream of air such as from an industrial smokestack.

Sewage. Refuse liquid or waste matter carried by sewers.

Smog. A visible mixture of solid, liquid, and gaseous air pollutants that are harmful both to human beings and to the environment.

Soil. A living system of weathered rock, organic matter, air, and water in which plants grow.

Sulfate. A salt of sulfuric acid.

Superfund. A federal government fund created for the identification and emergency cleanup of the nation's most toxic sites.

Toxic waste. The extremely dangerous by-product of chemical production or use.

Underground mining. The process of digging mines, often deep underground, usually for the purpose of obtaining coal or non-fuel minerals.

Urban sprawl. The spread of civilization out of urban and into rural areas.

Water pollution. The transfer of contaminating substances into water, usually as a result of human activities.

Water table. The highest level of a groundwater reservoir.

Weathering. The chemical decomposition or physical changing of rocks into smaller particles.

Wetlands. Land containing a high moisture content.

BIBLIOGRAPHY

"As Pollution Problems Spread, Communities Are Taking Action." *National Wildlife*, February/March 1989, p. 35.

As We Live and Breathe. Washington, D.C.: National Geographic Society, 1971.

Audette, Rose Marie. "Acid Rain Is Killing More than Lakes and Trees." *Environmental Action*, May/June 1987, p. 10.

Blair, William G. "Lung Peril Seen for Custodians." *New York Times*, May 6, 1990, p. 19-Y.

Budiansky, Stephen, and Robert F. Black. "Tons and Tons of Trash and No Place To Put It." *U.S. News and World Report*, Dec. 14, 1987, pp. 58 - 62.

Christrup, Judy. "Rising from the Ashes." *Greenpeace*, May/June 1988, p. 6.

"Deadlines Pass and a Rising Tide of Problems Remains Unsolved." *National Wildlife*, February/March 1989, p. 35.

D'Ella, Christopher F. "Nutrient Enrichment of the Chesapeake Bay: Too Much of a Good Thing." *Environment*, March 1987, p. 6.

The Earth Report. Los Angeles: Price Stern Sloan, Inc., 1988.

Grossman, Karl. *The Poison Conspiracy.* Sag Harbor, NY: The Permanent Press, 1983.

Lord, Deirdre. "Campus Life, Eco Dorms." *Environmental Action*, November/December 1988, p. 9.

Moran, Joseph M., Michael D. Morgan, and James H. Wiersma. *An Introduction to Environmental Sciences.* Boston: Little, Brown and Company, 1973.

"Public Safety/Private Greed." *Environmental Action*, September/October 1987, p. 11.

"Record Ozone Levels and an Acid Rain Stalemate Obscure Progress." *National Wildlife*, February/March 1989, p. 35.

Stiak, Jim. "When Toxics Reduce Recycling." *Environmental Action*, May/June 1987, p. 9.

Sullivan, Margaret. "Caution: Children at Play." *Environmental Action*, September/October 1987, p. 20.

Swanson, Stevenson. "Business Cleans up on Pollution." *Chicago Tribune*, April 18, 1990, p. 1.

Toner, Mike. "Pollution Fighters Take to the Trees." *National Wildlife*, December/January 1987, p. 38.

Wagner, Richard H. *Environment and Man.* New York: W. W. Norton & Co., Inc., 1974.

Wallace, David Rains. *Life in the Balance.* New York: Harcourt Brace Jovanovich, 1987.

Wolff, Anthony. "Dispatches: Boston's Toilet—The True Story." *Audubon*, March 1989, p. 26.

INDEX